AARVY AARDVARK
FINDS HOPE

A Read Aloud Story For People of All Ages
about
loving and losing,
friendship and hope.

WRITTEN BY DONNA O'TOOLE

ILLUSTRATED AND HAND LETTERED BY KORE LOY MCWHIRTER

MOUNTAIN RAINBOW PUBLICATIONS
Burnsville, North Carolina

Library of Congress Cataloging-in-Publication Data

O'Toole, Donna R., 1939—
    Aarvy Aardvark Finds Hope.

        Summary: With the help of his friend Ralphy Rabbit, Aarvy
Aardvark comes to terms with the loss of his mother and brother.
        [1. Loss (Psychology)—Fiction.   2. Death—Fiction.
3. Friendship—Fiction.   4. Aardvark—Fiction.   5. Rabbits—Fiction.]
    I. McWhirter, Kore Loy, ill.   II. Title.
    PZ7. 0877 Aar 1989   [E]   89-13629
    ISBN 1-878321-25-0

Published by

Mountain Rainbow Publications
a division of
Rainbow Connection
477 Hannah Branch Road
Burnsville, North Carolina, 28714
704-675-5909

6th Printing, 1997

ISBN 1-878321-25-0
LC   89-13629

To
my son
STEVEN SCHMIDT

and
to all the Ralphy Rabbits
who help
us heal and grow.

We welcome you to colour
the drawings in this book
in any way that pleases
you.

Kore Loy McWhirter
Donna O'Toole

CHAPTER 1

ALL ALONE

Aarvy Aardvark moved slowly across the clearing. It was a sunny day. Aarvy hadn't noticed.

Aarvy kept his snout to the ground. That snout was his friend. He could depend on it. He could depend on it to find food. He could depend on it to always be there.

But today even Aarvy's snout being there didn't help. It didn't comfort him and he wasn't using it to gather food. Aarvy wasn't hungry again today.

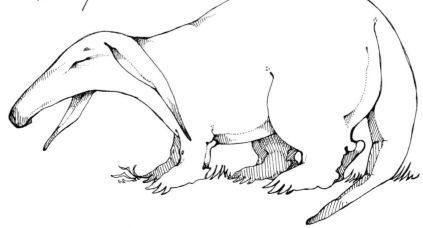

It all started when Aarvy's mother and his brother Varky were taken by some humans to a place called Zoo. Aarvy's mother had told him about that place. The humans had taken Aarvy's father there when Aarvy was barely knee-high to a baboon.

At first, Aarvy had been so lonely for Clarice and Varky that he cried all day long.

Lots of animals had come by to try to cheer Aarvy up. There were elephants and lions, a hippo and a gazelle. Even a giraffe and a rhino who lived far away joined the group that crowded around Aarvy.

They said they wanted to make Aarvy feel better.

But Aarvy didn't feel better.

Even with all the animals there, Aarvy felt all alone.

The giraffe asked Aarvy what
she could do to help.
　　But Aarvy couldn't tell her.
Aarvy didn't know.

"I know," said a big black buzzard who swooped down from his perch high above the others. The buzzard considered himself an expert on such things. "We don't have to worry,... he's doing just as is to be expected."

"You're depressed," he said to Aarvy. "Two months from now you'll feel angry, boy. Real angry. But as for now, you should talk to me. Get your feelings out. You've got to talk!"

Aarvy just stared. First at the buzzard, then at his dusty grey paws.

"It's better not to care so much," added a monkey who spoke quickly, then ran and hid behind the rhino.

"Be happy for them," said the laughing hyena. "They're in a better place now. They'll never ever have to dig for food again."

"Yeh, Aarvy," crooned in a mocking-bird. "You should remember the good times. Be glad you were with them as long as you were. Why, my mother left the nest the minute I learned to fly."

The buzzard jumped in again. "It's for your own good, boy. We're only trying to help. Get it out! Do it!"

But Aarvy couldn't do it.

Soon after that the buzzard left, ruffling his feathers and making sharp crackling sounds under his breath.

Later that day the other animals left too.

"We tried," Aarvy heard an elephant whisper as he passed. "We did our best," he heard the gazelle reply.

That made Aarvy feel even worse.

So today, in the clearing, Aarvy was all alone.

He was remembering what the mockingbird had said. He tried to remember the good times. He tried to remember rainbows. Aarvy had always loved rainbows. He had often told Clarice that someday he would climb one right to the top. Now he couldn't even remember their colors.

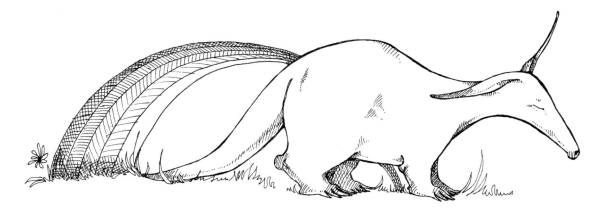

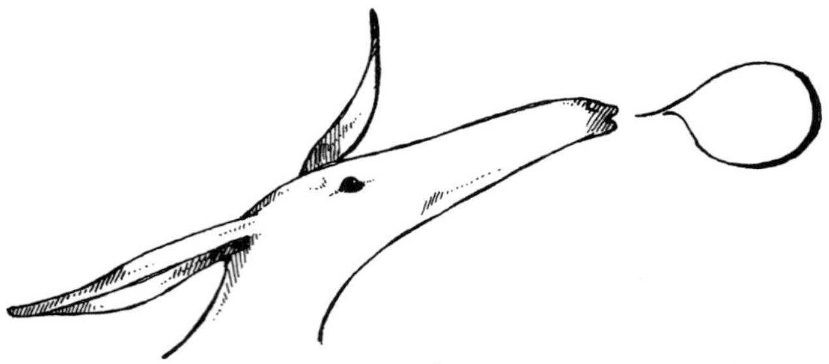

He even tried to remember playing
with Varky. Once he puckered up his
snout and tried to whistle the way he
and Varky had done when they played,
but

no

sound

came.

"Oh, what's the use," said
Aarvy Aardvark.
"I'll never have fun again anyway."

CHAPTER 2

RALPHY RABBiT

Aarvy found that Ralphy Rabbit was different from the other animals.

He was different because he didn't stay away. In fact, Ralphy Rabbit came back every day and sat beside Aarvy.

He would sit for hours.

Ralphy didn't seem to mind that Aarvy didn't talk.

"It's OK," he said. "When my sister Shai-le got caught in a trap, and I couldn't get her out, and she died, I couldn't talk about it either. Not for a long, long time."

Then he thumped the ground. When some ants came to the surface he used his paw to move them closer to Aarvy's snout. "Go ahead. Eat some, Aarvy. It's OK," he said.

When Aarvy moved so slowly that most of the ants ran away before he could eat them, Ralphy didn't even get mad. "You did fine, Aarvy, just fine!" he said. "Here, I'll help you find more."

Another day, even though Aarvy didn't ask, Ralphy told Aarvy more about his sister. "It was many years ago," Ralphy began, "but I still remember how bad I felt when Shai-le died."

"But now," he said, "I mostly remember how much fun we used to have."

"Sometimes, when I'm playing in the grass by the mud hole, or when a breeze tickles my fur — just so — I remember Shai-le. I remember how she loved to tease and play. She used to sneak up behind me and yell 'Boo!' or 'Duck quick!' or 'Watch out Ralphy — the sky is falling!' Then she'd run and hide."

As time went by Ralphy told many stories about playing with Shai-le. Ralphy told Aarvy how he could always find Shai-le when she hid. He would just wait very quietly outside the bushes for a long time. Then, all of a sudden, he'd thump wildly on the ground. Then he'd jump up and down, clap his paws and yell 'whoo eee, whoo eee, whoo eee, woo!.. woo!.. woo!..' over and over.

Pretty soon Shai-le would stick out one ear, then the other. Next she'd stick out her head. Then her leg. That's when Ralphy would make his move. Ralphy would make a giant rabbit leap and grab Shai-le's leg. Together they would fall down, rolling and laughing——over and over they'd go. Laughing all the way.

They'd laugh until their sides hurt.
They'd laugh until they could hardly move.
In fact, Ralphy and Shai-le even
laughed until they cried, just from the fun
of it!

"Are you sure Shai-le is really dead?"
Aarvy asked Ralphy one day. "Maybe she'll
come back some day."

Ralphy told Aarvy he was sure.

"How can you be sure about dead?"
asked Aarvy.

"I looked at her and I saw that she
wasn't breathing anymore," said Ralphy Rabbit.
"I spoke to her real loud, and she didn't talk
back. Then I touched the pink part of her ear
where she was ticklish and she didn't even
move. Mama said she would never hear or
talk or move again."

"At first I thought Shai-le was just sleeping. But Mama told me being dead isn't anything like being asleep.

"Then Mama told me that being dead doesn't hurt. See, being dead means you don't feel anything at all. And she told me being dead meant Shai-le would never eat or hop or play... ever again."

At first Aarvy felt sad when he heard Ralphy say all that. But his feelings changed when Ralphy said more. "But, you know what?" asked Ralphy Rabbit. "Sometimes I feel like Shai-le is really here. Not 'really' in the way grown-ups know it— in another way."

"Those times I feel like Shai-le is alive again in a different way. Like being alive inside my skin, instead of outside of it."

Ralphy told Aarvy that sometimes he even felt like Shai-le was laughing from somewhere deep inside himself.

That made him want to stretch. It tickled him. It felt so good that sometimes Ralphy would jump right up! He'd jump very high... until he'd feel like he was floating in a blue and purple and rainbow-colored sky.

When he'd come down again, Ralphy
Rabbit would feel warm all over. Like he'd
been hugged by all the animals
            and all the flowers
            and all the stars
            and all the planets
                in the whole universe.

"Sometimes," Ralphy said to Aarvy, "I still wish I could talk to Shai-le in the old way. But mostly I'm happy when I think about her."

"I'm happy because I can remember her. I can still feel her. She's a part of me. Forever and ever."

And Ralphy said that made him feel very full and very peaceful. "And," he said, kicking up his heels and clicking them in mid-air, "sometimes very playful too."

CHAPTER 3

A FRIENDSHIP GROWS

Aarvy Aardvark wasn't always sure he liked Ralphy Rabbit being around.

Sometimes, when he felt like crying, he'd feel embarrassed and want to be alone.

Then he'd get angry at Ralphy.

One day Aarvy was feeling so bad that he lifted his snout and bellowed,

"Why don't you just go home! You make me mad— always hanging around,

hanging around! Don't you have anything better to do, Ralphy Rabbit?

...STUPID RABBIT!"

So Ralphy Rabbit left for his home in the nearby brush. As Ralphy left, Aarvy clapped his paws together and snorted, "Good riddance to bad rabbits!"

But soon Aarvy felt even worse than before.

The next day the clouds hung low, like heavy grey curtains drawn over the sun. Aarvy lay in their shadow all day long.

He was tired. So tired that he barely moved. So tired that he didn't even open his eyes. But he couldn't sleep either. He didn't even daydream.

But several times he said to himself, "I just wish that I was dead."

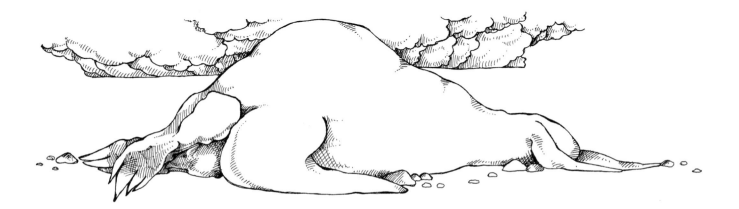

When Aarvy finally did open his eyes he saw the last glow of the setting sun break through the clouds. It was shining on Ralphy Rabbit's fur.

"Hello Aarvy," said Ralphy hopping closer. "I've been waiting for you. How about you and me heading out to dinner over by the old oak tree? I hear there's some mighty fine food there. Come, my friend, I'll lead the way."

And so, as the sun was setting and the moon rising, Ralphy Rabbit and Aarvy Aardvark went to eat.

     After that Ralphy and Aarvy looked for food and ate together every day.

     Ralphy would nibble on plants and flowers at the edge of the clearing while Aarvy would wave his thick snout back and forth over the sandy soil.

     At first Aarvy did more looking than eating. But one day, late that summer, Aarvy found a big ant hill and ate and ate and ate. He was surprised to find food tasted good again.

In the days that followed, Aarvy
would often eat his fill, roll over on his
back and look skyward. Aarvy would
lie for hours and hours watching the
flight of the blue birds that filled
the autumn skies. He would feel full
and rather contented.

But Aarvy never played.

"I should stop this silly daydreaming," he thought to himself one day. "What good does it do, anyway? And what good am I," he thought, "laying around doing nothing? Why I can't even whistle or kick up my heels like I did when—
When—"

All of a sudden Aarvy got a sharp feeling of sadness in his chest. A single tear rolled down each cheek.
"When—

When—

—When Varky and Mother were here," he said to himself, finally able to complete his thought.

It hurt to say their names, even to himself.

But somehow it also felt better. He hadn't thought of them in a long, long time.

"Mother and Varky...
Mother and Varky..."
He whispered their names again and again and again.
"Mother and Varky..." And twice he even whispered his mother's name.

"Varky and Clarice...
Varky and Clarice..."
He remembered that his mother had a beautiful-sounding name.

"**How dear they were!**" he said out loud, surprising himself.

"How near who were?" asked Ralphy Rabbit, who was hopping over to be closer to his friend Aarvy Aardvark.

"Dear, not near," said Aarvy, barely whispering again. And then he said, "I was thinking about them. I was thinking about Mother and Varky."

"Oh...," said Ralphy Rabbit, moving closer to Aarvy's side. "Yes, indeed. How dear and how near," he added.

Then they were both silent for a long time.

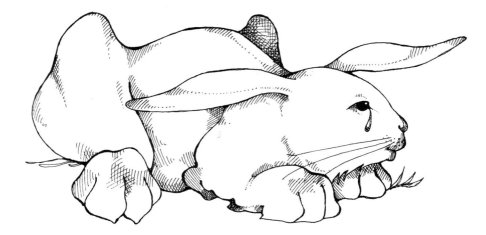

"Yes indeed," Aarvy finally said, shaking his head. "How dear and how near."

This time it was Ralphy Rabbit who had tears in his eyes. For although he hadn't seen a smile on Aarvy's face, he was quite certain that from someplace far away he had heard one begin to tiptoe into Aarvy's voice.

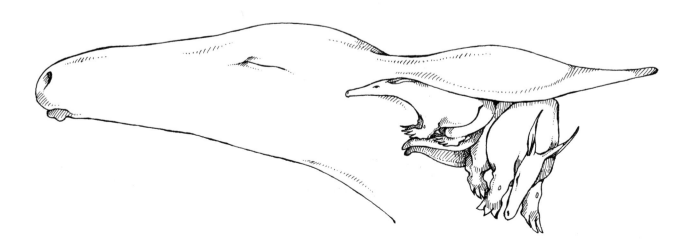

CHAPTER 4

WHAT AM I MEANT TO DO?

Time went by. The seasons changed several times. Aarvy continued to watch the blue birds.

Sometimes as he watched, Aarvy would lift his snout up off the ground. Then he'd wave it slowly through the air as if he too were flying.

"Flying is what birds are meant to do," Aarvy said to Ralphy one hot afternoon as they stretched out under the old oak. "And it must be fun for them."

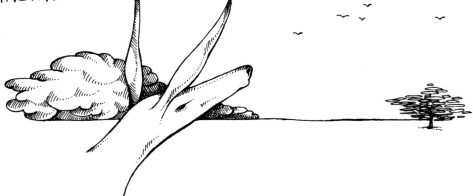

"Just like Varky and me," said Aarvy. "We were meant to use our legs to move around and gather food. And we had fun... sometimes."

"We whistled and snorted and zig-zagged across clearings. And sometimes we got so frisky that we forgot we were aardvarks, and we jumped right off the ground."

Ralphy Rabbit laughed. "The Flying Aardvarks!" he said. "You and Varky must have looked pretty funny with all four legs in the air."

"Tell me more stories, Aarvy," said Ralphy. "I like to hear you talk."

That afternoon Aarvy Aardvark talked and talked. He told many stories.

At first Ralphy kept his ears all the way up so he could hear every word Aarvy had to say. But as Aarvy talked on, Ralphy got sleepy. His ears drooped and he had to blink his eyes to keep them open.

Aarvy Aardvark was too busy talking to notice when Ralphy fell asleep. He was talking about whether or not animals were meant to have fun. That got him thinking about his mother, Clarice.

"Mother played," said Aarvy.

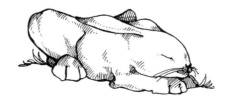

Aarvy remembered how Clarice had taken Varky and him out to whistle and dance and play in the moonlight. "She did funny side steps," said Aarvy. "And when Varky and I jumped, she whistled for us too."

Then he told the story about the time Clarice had tried to jump off the ground with them. But instead of going up she tripped over her snout and fell head over claws into a patch of daisies. "When she got up she had a daisy hanging from her ear, and she laughed and laughed. Varky and I laughed too," said Aarvy.

Aarvy blinked several times. The memory of his mother in the patch of yellow daisies was so strong that he could see her. He saw her in his imagination.

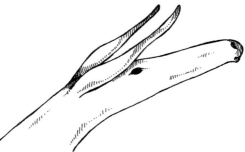

Then Aarvy remembered something else.

"The orange ribbon," he thought, jumping to his feet. "I had forgotten about the orange ribbon Mother always wore!"

Aarvy hung his head. "How could I have forgotten something we all loved so much?"

Then he added, "Too much... I've forgotten too much."

Suddenly the memory of the blue birds came to him again. "Birds do have fun," he thought with certainty.

"And they do feel free....
And once—
A long time ago—
I DID TOO! I FELT FREE TO PLAY!"

He said it very loud!

"Felt free to what?" asked Ralphy. He had bolted wide awake at the sound of Aarvy's loud voice.

"TO PLAY!" yelled Aarvy. "Free to play! I was once, you know! I was remembering."

"Ohh!" said Ralphy Rabbit. "Well then, let's do it again. Let's play Hide the Wild Carrot Root, or Wise Owl Says, or Pin the Tail on—"

"Naw," interrupted Aarvy. "I've forgotten all those silly games. I'd rather just lie here and watch the blue birds fly. You go ahead, Ralphy. You play. Do that jig you do. I'll watch you, too."

"Alright," said Ralphy. His voice had grown soft and slow. "But, dear Aarvy, I wish you would play."
"Someday I hope we **can** play together, my friend."

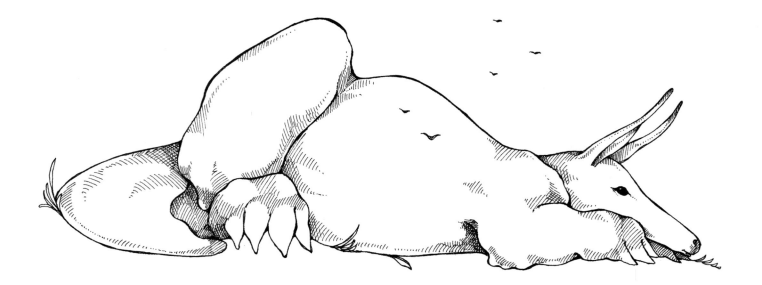

And so it was.

Aarvy would lie on his back. Then Aarvy would lie on his side. He watched the birds flying above. He watched his friend Ralphy Rabbit hop and sing and do the Wild Irish Carrot Jig.

Once Aarvy got so caught up in the movement that he puckered up his snout, in much the same way he used to when he whistled, and a sound came out.

"WHEW..E..e..e!"

Aarvy was so surprised that he nearly jumped up.

"Maybe I **could** whistle again," thought Aarvy.

"Perhaps, some day."

CHAPTER 5

DANCING WITH FEELINGS

The next season that passed was a long wet season.

During the rains Aarvy had spent a lot of time inside getting his house in order.

He listened to the sound of the wind as it played with the rain. He listened to the rain playing with the bushes. He played Animal Dominoes and Spill-the-Pebbles with his friend Ralphy Rabbit, and they talked and talked.

One afternoon, Aarvy told Ralphy about the time he had puckered up his snout and had almost whistled. "At first, after I did it, I felt really good," Aarvy said. "But later I felt bad."

After that, Aarvy and Ralphy talked late into the night about feelings.

Often when Aarvy was alone, he would sit at the entrance to his burrow, looking out over the grassland. He would imagine he was a tiny dot of white light floating through the sky.

It gave Aarvy a marvelous feeling, for he discovered that in his mind he could travel anywhere he wanted. He discovered he could **be** anything at all! After a while, Aarvy also discovered he no longer felt guilty about feeling good.

Sometimes, in his imagination, he changed from a dot of white light into a whole sky of white light. Then the sky full of white light changed into a color. Then he fell to earth as a tree or a flower or a green and purple butterfly.

"It makes me feel like I'm OK," he said to Ralphy. "Like I fit into things."

Today Aarvy was back in the clearing. The rain had stopped, and he was looking for food. He wasn't finding much to eat, so Aarvy wandered farther and farther away from his usual feeding ground.

Suddenly he saw a small speck of blue lying in the grass just ahead of him. Aarvy's curiosity moved him cautiously forward until he was standing above the blue object.

It was a bird, lying very still.

It was mostly blue. But on its wings were the most beautiful bright orange bands Aarvy had ever seen.

The breeze was blowing the bird's feathers ever so slightly. And with the light shining on them, they looked even more beautiful than the dewdrops Aarvy had seen on the grass in the morning sun.

Aarvy walked as quietly around the blue bird as he could, hoping not to startle or waken it.

The blue bird didn't make a sound.

It didn't move or fly away.

Aarvy sat down, spellbound by its beauty.

As Aarvy sat watching the still blue bird with the orange wing bands, he remembered lying in the clearing watching the birds fly and play in the sky.

After a long time of silence, Aarvy spoke to the blue bird. He spoke very softly. To his amazement, he said "I love you."

Aarvy didn't understand why he had said "I love you" to the blue bird. But he didn't worry about why. The words came from something stirring deep inside him.

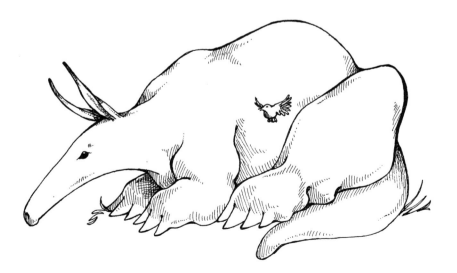

Aarvy remembered the evening that he and Ralphy had talked about feelings.

"Lots of animals don't trust their feelings, or they're scared of them," Ralphy had said. But I think feelings are a gift. They are friends that can help us. And they're always there—because they live right inside us. They might be painful or shake us up at times, but, if we listen to them, they will tell us what we need so we can heal and grow."

"The thing to do with feelings," said Ralphy with a twinkle in his eyes, "is to invite them to come outside in the open so we can dance with them."

Aarvy Aardvark liked what Ralphy had said about feelings, but he didn't understand it all. Especially the part about dancing with them.

He sure didn't feel like dancing right now. In fact, he didn't know **what** he was feeling.

What Aarvy **did** know was that, for now at least, there were no more words he wanted to say.

He knew he wanted to stay with the blue bird with the orange wing bands — perhaps forever.

So Aarvy stayed, sitting quietly by its side.

He just sat there and waited.

As Aarvy waited he began to cry. Then he thought,

My beautiful bird,
My beautiful bird,
How I do love you,
My beautiful bird.

Aarvy forgot all about eating. He forgot all about the music the wind makes during a storm. And Aarvy forgot all about what time it was getting to be.

CHAPTER 6

SAYING GOODBYE

When it was late afternoon, Ralphy began looking around for his good friend Aarvy Aardvark.

It had become a habit for them to walk home together. Although they often didn't talk as they moved across the grasslands, just being together made their day feel more complete.

And so, as the sun was beginning to sink low in the sky, Ralphy Rabbit found his friend Aarvy Aardvark. Aarvy was sitting beside the blue bird with the orange wing bands. Sitting silently with tears running down his cheeks.

"Such a beautiful one," said Ralphy
to Aarvy as he placed his paw gently on
Aarvy's knee.

"How did she die, my friend?" he
asked quietly.

"Die!!

"Die...?" said Aarvy.

Aarvy was silent for a long time.
"I... I... don't know," he finally said.
"I found her lying very still. Her feathers
were catching the breeze. And the
sun's light was like dewdrops on her orange
wing bands. I have waited a long time for
her to rise up. I wanted to see her fly."
"I thought maybe if I waited long
enough, she'd come back home with me."

Aarvy's words rushed out of him like a stream breaking through a dam. Then he whispered, "I loved her," wondering if his friend would laugh at him.

"Of course," said Ralphy Rabbit. "Of course you loved her. And perhaps you still do."

Aarvy felt relieved. There was not a trace of mockery or sarcasm in in his friend's voice, only kindness— and some sadness too.

"But she is dead, my friend," said Ralphy Rabbit.

"What we have to do now is to find a way we can remember her and her beauty. That way we'll have her inside of us. The memories can help us grow. We need that, Aarvy, because you and I are alive. We have to remember that, and not be ashamed."

"Come, my friend," said Ralphy Rabbit, touching his paw to Aarvy's. "We'll bury her."

The sun was just beginning to set as Aarvy Aardvark and Ralphy Rabbit finished digging in the ground, which was still moist from the many days of rain. Aarvy's strong legs and firm claws could have made digging such a small hole an easy job. But Aarvy was digging very slowly.

"It's hard work," said Aarvy.

"Yes," said Ralphy, "but it's good work."

Ralphy picked green leaves one by
one from a nearby bush to line the grave.
He chose only the prettiest ones.

Aarvy helped arrange the leaves.
They placed them close together like a
thick, woven carpet.

Before they placed the blue bird onto the green leaves, Aarvy said, "Would it be OK to give her a name?"

"Yes... yes indeed," said Ralphy. "But what name?"

"Can we remember her as Clarice?" asked Aarvy. "It's a beautiful name."

Tears came into Ralphy's eyes. He looked at his friend and nodded slowly. "I like that, Aarvy. It's a fine idea."

"Goodbye, beautiful Clarice," said Ralphy. "Goodbye."

Together Aarvy and Ralphy placed
Clarice the bird into the hole in the ground.
They laid green leaves over her blue and
orange feathers. Then Ralphy stepped back.
He looked at Aarvy. He was waiting.

"You have to say goodbye, Aarvy," he said. "It's very hard, but you have to. If we never say goodbye, we never find out how to go on. Not really. And if we can't go on, how can we ever show others how beautiful Clarice was?"

"Saying goodbye doesn't mean you have to forget Clarice, Aarvy," Ralphy said gently.

"It means you accept what is. Then you'll be free to remember without it hurting so much. By letting go of Clarice you'll find you have more energy for living. You might even find that saying goodbye helps you love yourself and others more than before. I think Clarice would like that, Aarvy."

Aarvy just looked at his friend Ralphy Rabbit. He felt a little confused. But he trusted Ralphy, and inside himself Ralphy's words felt comfortable.

Aarvy nodded.

"Come, my friend," said Ralphy.
"Let us sing."

It wasn't easy, but they did sing.
They sang,

Clarice — Clarice
oh beautiful one
you lived
you played
you flyed
you died,
Clarice — Clarice ...

They sang it many times. They didn't
count how many. After a while they found
themselves being very still again.

CHAPTER 7

SOMEDAY SOON

It was Aarvy Aardvark who pushed the first clump of dirt into the grave.

Aarvy was crying, but he didn't feel weak. He felt strong. Stronger than he could ever remember feeling.

He could sing to Clarice. He could sing. Imagine!

In a fleeting thought he wondered how it would feel to whistle again. To whistle... and maybe even to jump again.

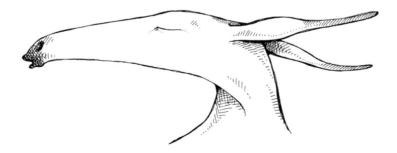

Aarvy looked at Ralphy Rabbit.
Ralphy was crying too.   But when Ralphy
looked at Aarvy they both smiled—right
through their tears.
        They stood very close together...
paw to paw.

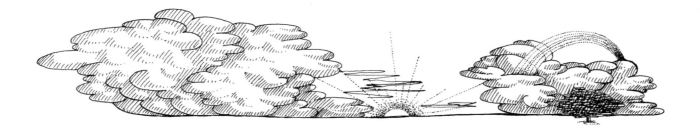

"We'd better go now," said Ralphy.

As Ralphy and Aarvy lifted their heads they saw the sky aglow with the last colors made by the setting sun.

It made Aarvy think about rainbows and their beautiful colors. He could remember every one.

Then he remembered something that until that very moment he had forgotten. He remembered that Clarice had told him that rainbows happen when the weather is changing.

"Tomorrow," said Aarvy, when they were almost to their homes, "tomorrow I will start practicing my whistling."

"And perhaps...

"Perhaps someday soon I will play again."

Then he turned his head toward Ralphy Rabbit. "Perhaps, someday soon, we will play together."

"Yes indeed," said Ralphy Rabbit.
"Yes indeed."

THE END.

and of course

THE BEGINNING........

THANKS TO THE ANIMALS

Facing loss and grief
isn't easy, so most of us find it easier
to do it indirectly. That's why animals
rather than people were used in this story.

Animals give us so much
and ask so little. Please
cherish the animals in your life and
treat them in gentle, conscious, life-
giving ways.

"Thanks to the Animals!"

ABOUT THE ILLUSTRATOR

Kore Loy McWhirter lives in the valley where she grew up, across the river from Donna O'Toole.

She likes to draw, paint in fresco, egg tempera and water-colour, make masks and tiles, and work with her mother the potter. When she's not doing artwork she also likes to write poems, sing, dance, be with her womyn-friends and chase around with her daughters megan and eliza.

Loy and her friends Jon and Bruce garden, build their house, raise their daughters, work for peace and play music together.

ABOUT THE AUTHOR

Donna O'Toole is a writer, counselor and teacher. She has taught courses in communication, counseling skills and loss and grief in colleges and universities in Michigan and North Carolina and conducts workshops on these topics throughout the United States and Canada.

She has directed Lapeer Area Hospice, The Michigan Bereavement Project and a statewide program for parents of terminally ill children. Her honors and awards include The Governor of Michigan's Volunteer of the Year Award and delegate to the White House Conference on Handicapping Conditions. She was awarded the Presidential Award of Excellence in Training from the National Hospice Organization for her book, **Bridging The Bereavement Gap**.

She considers the death of Caren, an infant daughter, the chronic illness and death of Matthew, a 21 year old son, coupled with the parenting of Steven, her greatest sources of learning, challenge and growth.

She lives in Celo Community in the mountains of North Carolina with her husband and best friend, Ron, where she is the founder and director of Rainbow Connection, a networking, resourcing, and training firm dedicated to helping people grow through change.

Aarvy's Story Now Available in Video

This moving story about loving and losing, friendship and hope comes to life through the incredible life size action puppets of artist-performer Bonnie Blue.

- Narrated by Donna O'Toole.
- Equisitely filmed by Ironwood Productions.
- Directed by award winning film maker Danny Miller.
- Original music by Ron Clearfield.

Donna O'Toole's
Aarvy Aardvark Finds Hope

A Story Of Hope For All Ages

Featuring the incredible
Bonnie Blue Puppets

45 minutes – Full color

We Have Many Exceptional Resources

We publish only materials that sing out hope without denying that life as a journey has both challenge and choice. We specialize in gathering and distributing over 400 books, audios and videos to help people grow through loss, change and grief. For a free copy of our mail order catalog, to order more Aarvy books, the video, audio cassette or teacher's guide to *Aarvy Aardvark Find's Hope*, call or write: Compassion Press, 477 Hannah Branch Road, Burnsville, North Carolina 28714, (704) 675-5909.